CRUISE SHIPS

amazing ships · amazing ships

JONATHAN SUTHERLAND AND DIANE CANWELL

Gareth Stevens
Publishing

Please visit our web site at: **www.garethstevens.com**
For a free color catalog describing Gareth Stevens Publishing's list of
high-quality books, call 1-800-542-2595 (USA) or 1-800-387-3178 (Canada).

Library of Congress Cataloging-in-Publication Data

Sutherland, Jonathan.
 Cruise ships / Jonathan Sutherland and Diane Canwell.
  p. cm. — (Amazing ships)
 ISBN: 978-0-8368-8378-7 (lib. bdg)
 1. Cruise ships. 2. Ocean liners.] I. Canwell, Diane. II. Title.
 VM381.S88 2008
 623.82'432—dc22   2007017050

This North American edition first published in 2008 by
Gareth Stevens Publishing
A Weekly Reader® Company
1 Reader's Digest Road
Pleasantville, NY 10570-7000 USA

Produced by Amber Books Ltd., Bradley's Close,
74–77 White Lion Street, London N1 9PF, U.K.

Project Editor: James Bennett
Copy Editors: Natasha Reed, Chris McNab
Design: Colin Hawes

Gareth Stevens managing editor: Mark Sachner
Gareth Stevens editor: Alan Wachtel
Gareth Stevens art direction: Tammy West
Gareth Stevens production: Jessica Yanke

All illustrations courtesy of Art-Tech/Aerospace

Photo credits: 5: Cody Images, 7: Photoshot (UPPA), 8: Getty Images (Henry Ray Abrams), 11: Popperfoto, 13: Cody Images, 15: Cody Images, 17: Popperfoto, 19: Mercy Ships International, 21: Cody Images, 23: Photoshot (World Pictures), 25: Antti Havukainen, 27: Windstar Cruises, 29: Regent Seven Seas Cruises

Printed in the United States of America

1 2 3 4 5 6 7 8 9 11 10 09 08 07

RMS Mauretania

The RMS *Mauretania* was launched in Newcastle upon Tyne, England, in September 1906. Her maiden voyage took place the following November, and she became one of the most luxurious and fastest **cruise ships** on the oceans. The *Mauretania* served until 1934, when she was finally retired because her owner brought in larger, faster vessels.

The ship's **steam turbine** engines produced 68,000 **horsepower** and could push the ship to a speed of 25 **knots** (46 kilometers per hour).

Passenger **berth**

Two of the ship's four screw propellers

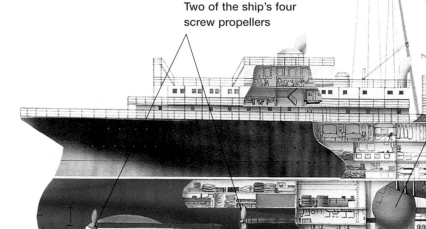

• The *Mauretania* won the Blue Riband award in September 1909 for the fastest transatlantic crossing. It remained hers until the German ship *Bremen* broke the record in 1929.

• The ship could carry up to 2,165 passengers: 563 in first-class, 464 in second-class, and 1,138 in third-class.

The ship could carry up to 6,000 tons of coal in this hold.

The **bridge**, from where the ship was piloted

In July 1935, the *Mauretania* headed for the breaker's yard at Rosyth, Scotland. All her furnishings had been sold.

The total length of the ship's **hull** was 790 feet (240 meters).

MAURETANIA

RMS Titanic

The RMS *Titanic* was a legendary superliner built at the Harland and Wolff shipyard in Belfast, Northern Ireland. Her career ended on April 14, 1912, on her maiden voyage from Europe to New York. She hit an iceberg that slashed open her hull, and she sank in just two hours and 40 minutes.

The *Titanic* had bronze three-bladed propellers at the sides and a single bronze four-bladed propeller in the center.

Main rear first-class staircase

One of the three massive Harland and Wolff engines

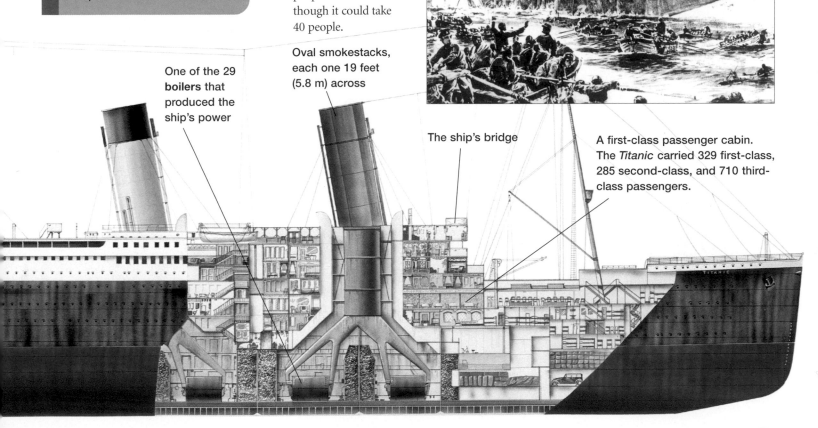

Did You Know?

The *Titanic* was said to be "practically unsinkable." Her hull had two separate walls and was divided into 16 watertight compartments.

It took 80 minutes to lower the *Titanic's* 20 lifeboats. Not all were full. For example, Lifeboat No.1 was launched with only 12 people on board even though it could take 40 people.

One of the 29 **boilers** that produced the ship's power

Oval smokestacks, each one 19 feet (5.8 m) across

The ship's bridge

A first-class passenger cabin. The *Titanic* carried 329 first-class, 285 second-class, and 710 third-class passengers.

AMERIGO VESPUCCI

The *Amerigo Vespucci* was launched from Castellamare di Stabia, Italy, in 1931. This Italian ship still sails today as a training vessel for the Italian Navy. She was built in the style of an eighteenth-century 74-cannon warship. Unlike those sailing ships, she also has engines. Her home port is Livorno, Italy.

This picture shows the *Amerigo Vespucci* sailing into New York in 1976. In 2002, she voyaged around the world.

Did You Know?

Italian mapmaker and explorer Amerigo Vespucci lived from 1454 to 1512. Many people believe that the Americas were named after him.

KEY FACTS

- Using her engines, *Amerigo Vespucci*'s top speed is 10 knots (18.5 kilometers per hour).

- She has a **draft** of about 23 feet (7 m).

- She has 26 sails and 18 miles (29 km) of rigging.

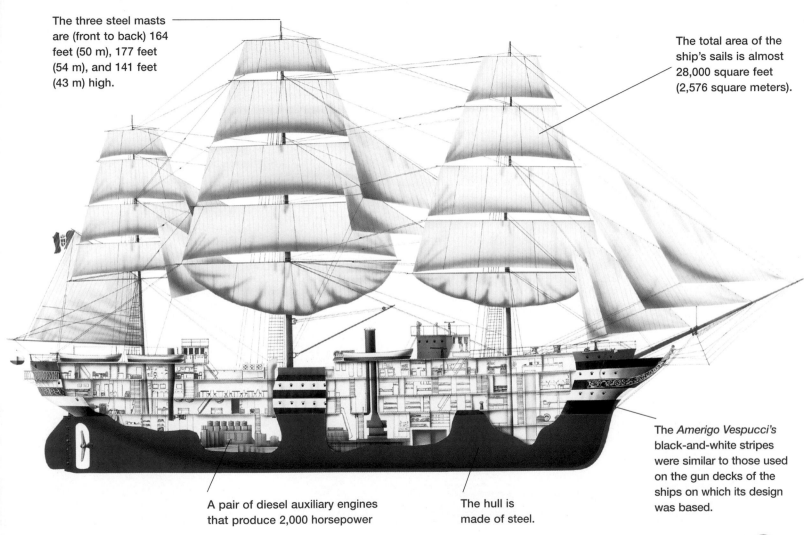

The three steel masts are (front to back) 164 feet (50 m), 177 feet (54 m), and 141 feet (43 m) high.

The total area of the ship's sails is almost 28,000 square feet (2,576 square meters).

A pair of diesel auxiliary engines that produce 2,000 horsepower

The hull is made of steel.

The *Amerigo Vespucci's* black-and-white stripes were similar to those used on the gun decks of the ships on which its design was based.

SS NORMANDIE

The SS *Normandie* was built in Saint Nazaire, France, in 1932. At the time, she was the fastest and the largest ship in the world. In 1942, at the New York Passenger Ship Terminal, she caught fire, **capsized**, and sank. She was being converted into a wartime troopship at the time. Several attempts were made to salvage and refit her, but all ultimately failed. She was finally scrapped in 1946.

This smokestack did not really work. It was there to make the ship look more balanced.

One of four turbo-electric engines, which together produced between 160,000 and 200,000 horsepower

The *Nomandie's* propellers weighed 23 tons (20.9 metric tons) each.

The main mast

An upper-deck passenger cabin. The ship could carry 1,972 passengers.

The SS *Normandie* was the largest ship in the world for five years. She was the first cruise ship to exceed 1,000 feet (305 m) in length.

The ship's bridge

RMS QUEEN MARY

The British cruise ship RMS *Queen Mary* was launched in September 1934. She sailed the North Atlantic Ocean from 1936 until she was finally retired from service in 1967. She is now a floating hotel, restaurant, and museum off Long Beach, California.

This steam turbine produced 160,000 horsepower. The ship's top speed was 32.6 knots (60 kph).

Each lifeboat could hold 145 people.

Four propeller shafts (two on each side)

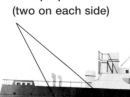

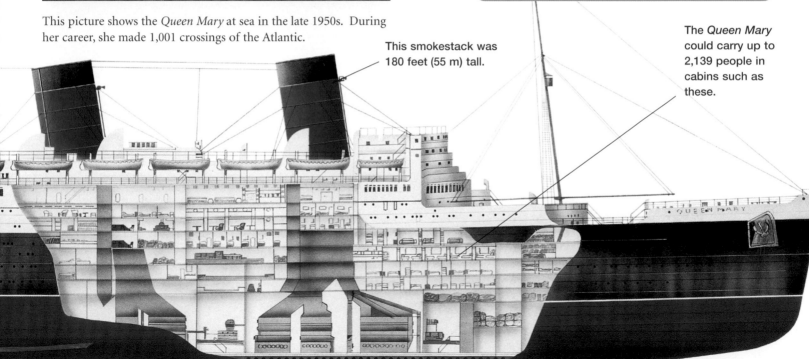

KEY FACTS

• The RMS *Queen Mary* made her maiden voyage from Southampton, England, on May 27, 1936.

• The *Queen Mary* won the Blue Riband prize in 1936 and 1938. Her 1938 speed record held until 1952, with an average speed of 31.69 knots (58.6 kph) on the eastbound Atlantic crossing.

This picture shows the *Queen Mary* at sea in the late 1950s. During her career, she made 1,001 crossings of the Atlantic.

This smokestack was 180 feet (55 m) tall.

The *Queen Mary* could carry up to 2,139 people in cabins such as these.

NIEUW AMSTERDAM

The Dutch ship *Nieuw Amsterdam* was launched in 1937. She was one the world's most luxurious cruise ships of the time. Because of World War II, she was converted to a troopship in 1940. She returned to the Netherlands in April 1946 and was reconverted to a passenger ship.

Did You Know?

After the war, it took 18 months to repair the ship. More than 378,000 soldiers had sailed on her, and many had scratched their names into her woodwork.

The hull of the ship was 758 feet (231 m) from **bow** to **stern**.

Steam turbines drove two propellers with 34,000 horsepower.

A first-class cabin. The ship had room for 556 first-class, 445 tourist-class, and 209 third-class passengers.

The *Nieuw Amsterdam* steams out of New York Harbor. Her hull was painted gray in the late 1950s when she was updated.

Vehicle storage deck

SS Rex

The SS *Rex* was an Italian-built ocean liner that was launched in 1931. She sailed on her maiden voyage out of Genoa, Italy, in September 1932, but only made it to Gibraltar, in the western Mediterranean Sea, before breaking down. She captured the famed Blue Riband award in August 1933 with an average speed to the United States of 28.92 knots (52.3 kph). The *Rex* was destroyed during World War II.

The *Rex*'s great speed was delivered by four huge propellers, two on each side.

Luxury cabin. The *Rex* had a capacity of 604 first-class, 378 second-class, 410 tourist-class, and 861 third-class passengers.

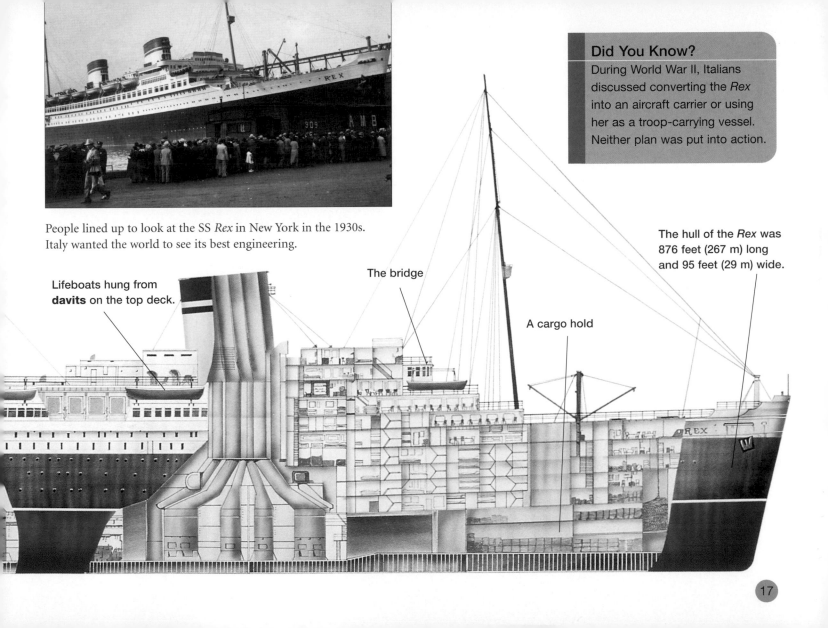

People lined up to look at the SS *Rex* in New York in the 1930s. Italy wanted the world to see its best engineering.

Did You Know?
During World War II, Italians discussed converting the *Rex* into an aircraft carrier or using her as a troop-carrying vessel. Neither plan was put into action.

The hull of the *Rex* was 876 feet (267 m) long and 95 feet (29 m) wide.

The bridge

Lifeboats hung from **davits** on the top deck.

A cargo hold

ANASTASIS

The *Victoria* was built as a cruise ship in Italy in 1953. In 1978, she was bought by Mercy Ships, a charitable organization, renamed the *Anastasis*, and turned into a medical vessel. Since then, she has delivered aid to some of the world's poorest countries.

Did You Know?
Mercy Ships is an organization that takes special medical ships to the world's poorest countries.

A cargo hold. The *Anastasis* has a cargo capacity of 1,500 tons (1,361 metric tons).

The ship's main cabin areas were converted into wards, with beds for the patients.

A pair of 8,050 horsepower Fiat 7510 engines

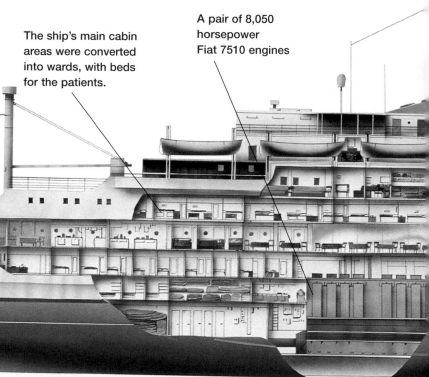

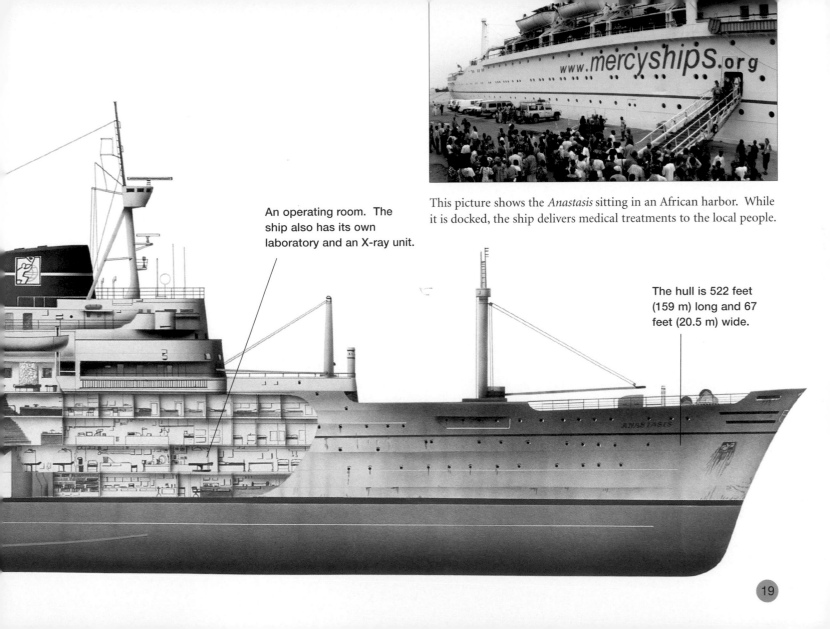

An operating room. The ship also has its own laboratory and an X-ray unit.

This picture shows the *Anastasis* sitting in an African harbor. While it is docked, the ship delivers medical treatments to the local people.

The hull is 522 feet (159 m) long and 67 feet (20.5 m) wide.

SS CANBERRA

The SS *Canberra* was built in Belfast, Northern Ireland, in 1960, and entered service the following year. She operated between 1961 and 1997. The *Canberra* was originally designed to serve as a passenger liner between Great Britain and Australia, but she was converted into a luxury cruise ship in 1974.

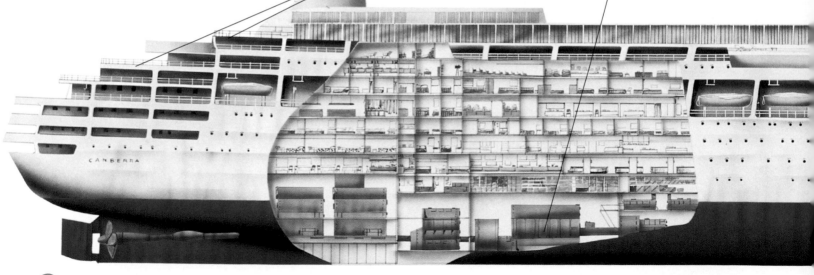

Both of these decks featured outdoor swimming pools.

One of the ship's main engines. The *Canberra* had two steam-turbine-driven 6,000-volt electric motors.

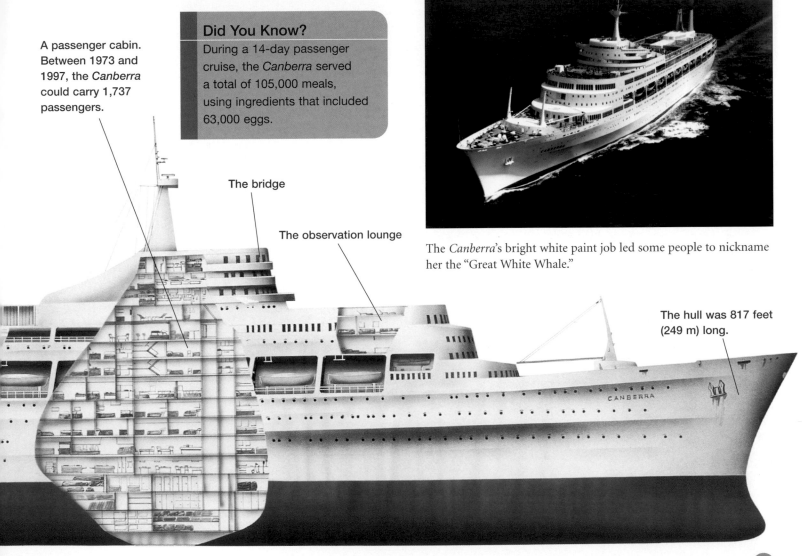

A passenger cabin. Between 1973 and 1997, the *Canberra* could carry 1,737 passengers.

The bridge

The observation lounge

The hull was 817 feet (249 m) long.

The *Canberra*'s bright white paint job led some people to nickname her the "Great White Whale."

CANBERRA

RMS Queen Elizabeth 2

The *Queen Elizabeth 2*, nicknamed the *QE2*, was launched in September 1967. She was the flagship of the Cunard Shipping Company from 1969 to 2004. The *QE2* was the last oil-burning passenger steamship to cross the Atlantic Ocean on regular runs. In 1982, she was refitted with diesel-powered engines. The *QE2* still sails on world tours. She operates out of Southampton, England.

The QE2's total height to the top of this funnel is 171 feet (52 m).

Engine room. The *QE2* has nine nine-cylinder, **turbocharged** diesel engines.

One of a pair of five-bladed propellers

- The *QE2* is one of the fastest passenger ships in use.

- The ship's synagogue is the only room left unchanged since 1969. Other facilities include five restaurants and a 485-seat movie theater.

The *QE2* has a steel hull, but, to reduce the ship's weight, much of her **superstructure** is made of aluminum.

A passenger cabin. The *QE2* can carry up to 1,892 passengers.

A cargo hold. The *QE2* has six huge cargo holds.

Did You Know?

By 2002, the *QE2* had sailed 5 million miles (8 million km). In a typical year, she sails once around the world and makes 30 transatlantic crossings.

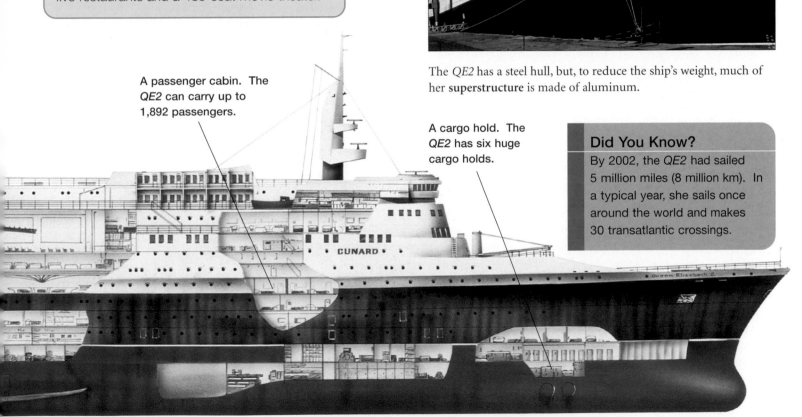

Silja Serenade

The *Silja Serenade* is a cruise ferry. She was delivered to the Finnish Silja Line Company in November 1990. At that time, she operated between Helsinki, Finland, and Stockholm, Sweden. Beginning in 1993, she sailed mostly from Turku and Mariehamn, in Finland, to Stockholm. In 1995, she switched back to her original route but kept Mariehamn as a stop.

Did You Know?
The ship has its own shopping "street" with eight different shops. Also on board are a sauna and jacuzzi, three restaurants, and a casino.

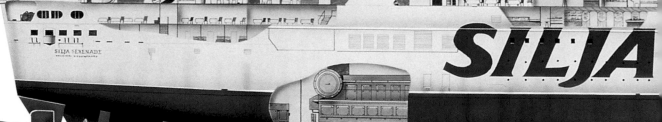

Passenger cabin. The ship has cabins for 986 passengers and a total capacity of 2,852 passengers.

The total length of the hull is 666 feet (203 m).

One of the ship's two propellers. The ship has a top speed of 21.5 knots (399 kph).

SILJA SERENADE

SILJA

- The voyage from Stockholm, Sweden, to Helsinki, Finland, takes about 16 hours.

- She was built at the Masa Yards, located in Turku, Finland.

- She carries more than 500,000 passengers every year.

Sundeck and moonlight **promenade**

The *Silja Serenade* is often described as a floating city, because she has a glass-roofed promenade lined with shops, cafés, and restaurants.

Vehicle deck. The *Silja Serenade* can carry up to 395 passenger cars.

25

WIND SURF

The *Wind Surf* was first known as the *Club Med 1*. Built in France in 1990, she was designed as a luxury cruise ship for the Club Med vacation company. In 1998, she was acquired by Windstar Cruises and renamed *Wind Surf*. She now operates in the Caribbean in the winter and in the Mediterranean in the summer.

Did You Know?

The *Wind Surf* has a draft of about 17 feet (5.2 m). This allows her to fit into ports that are too small for larger ships.

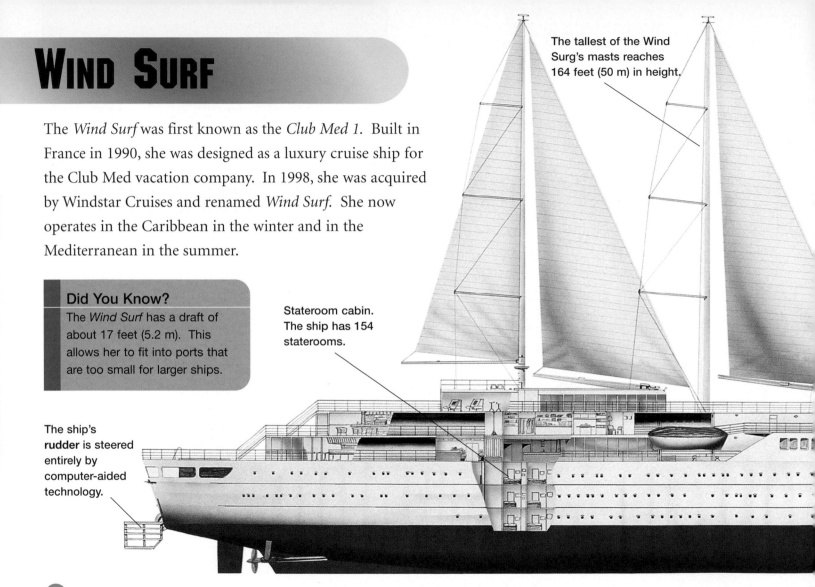

The tallest of the Wind Surg's masts reaches 164 feet (50 m) in height.

Stateroom cabin. The ship has 154 staterooms.

The ship's **rudder** is steered entirely by computer-aided technology.

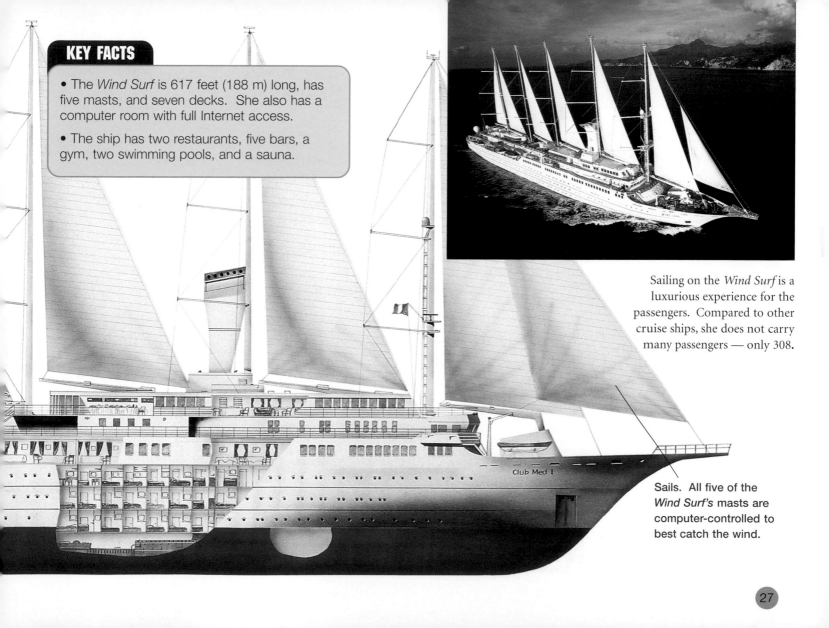

KEY FACTS

• The *Wind Surf* is 617 feet (188 m) long, has five masts, and seven decks. She also has a computer room with full Internet access.

• The ship has two restaurants, five bars, a gym, two swimming pools, and a sauna.

Sailing on the *Wind Surf* is a luxurious experience for the passengers. Compared to other cruise ships, she does not carry many passengers — only 308.

Club Med 1

Sails. All five of the *Wind Surf's* masts are computer-controlled to best catch the wind.

ASIA STAR

The *Asia Star* was called the *Radisson Diamond* until she was bought by Asia Cruises and renamed. Built in 1992 at the Rauma Yards in Finland, she has a special design called Small Waterplane Area Twin Hull (SWATH) that allows her to be large but not heavy. The *Asia Star* weighs 20,295 tons (18,416 metric tons).

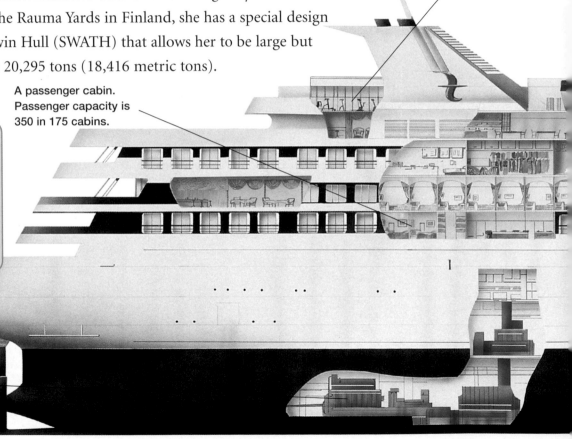

Gymnasium

A passenger cabin. Passenger capacity is 350 in 175 cabins.

KEY FACTS

• The *Asia Star* is the world's largest **catamaran**, or twin-hulled ship.

• The *Asia Star*'s main entertainment area is two decks high and has a grand staircase, a large dance floor, and a theatrical stage.

The ship's hull is 430 feet (131 m) long.

In the engine room, her eight-cylinder and six-cylinder diesel engines produce a total of 15,000 horsepower.

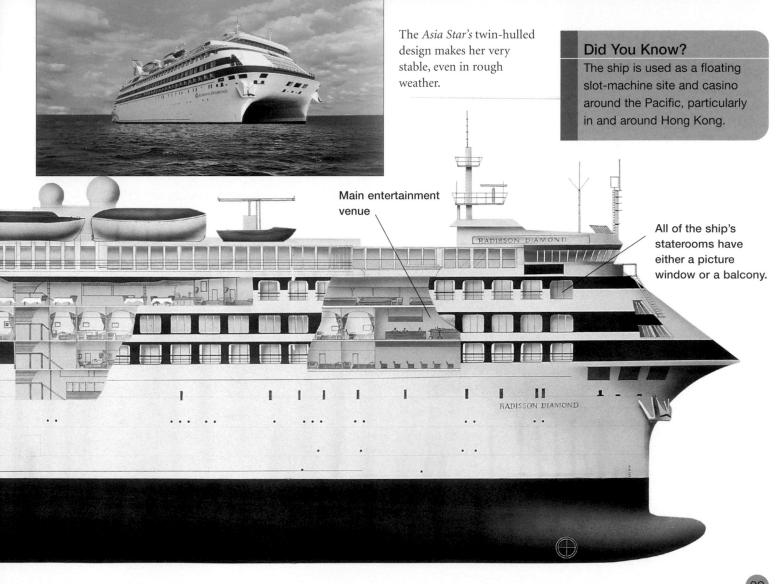

The *Asia Star's* twin-hulled design makes her very stable, even in rough weather.

Main entertainment venue

All of the ship's staterooms have either a picture window or a balcony.

RADISSON DIAMOND

RADISSON DIAMOND

GLOSSARY

berth a place to sleep on board a ship or other vehicle

boiler a device for making high-pressure steam that can be used to provide power for running an engine or machine

bow the front part of a ship

bridge the part of a ship where the navigation and steering equipment is usually found and from where the ship is controlled

capsize to overturn in the water

catamaran a boat or ship with two parallel hulls

cruise ship a ship designed purely for vactions, with entertainment for the passengers provided during the voyage

davit a crane that extends over the side of a ship

draft the depth that the lowest part of a ship reaches beneath the surface of the water

horsepower a unit of measurement for the power of an engine

hull the main body of a ship that is built to allow it to float

knot a unit for measurment for the speed of ships that is equivalent to 1.15 miles per hour (1.8 kph)

promenade a walkway, usually around the main deck of a ship, on which passengers can stand or walk

rudder a hinged device fitted at the rear of a ship that hangs in the water and is used to guide the ship in a particular direction

steam turbine a type of engine that uses superheated steam to provide power

stern the rear part of a ship

superstructure all the parts of the ship above the main deck

turbocharged having a system found in some engines that increases the power the engine can generate

FOR MORE INFORMATION

BOOKS

- *Mega Book of Ships.* Lynne Gibbs (Chrysalis Children's Books)

- *The Great Ships.* Patrick O'Brien (Walker Books)

- *The Sinking of the Titanic.* Matt Doeden (Capstone Press)

- *The Sinking of the Titanic.* Monumental Milestones in Modern History (series). Jim Whiting (Mitchell Lane Publishing)

- *Titanic: A Primary Source History.* In Their Own Words (series). Seanan Molony (World Almanac® Library)

WEB SITES

- Monsters of the Sea—The Great Ocean Liners of Time *www.ocean-liners.com*

- RMS Titanic Inc *www.rmstitanic.net*

- Cunard (owners of Queen Mary II, Queen Elizabeth II and Queen Victoria) *www.cunard.com*

- Cruise Ship Odyssey *www.cruiseshipodyssey.com*

Publisher's note to educators and parents:

Our editors have carefully reviewed these Web sites to ensure that they are suitable for children. Many web sites change frequently, however, and we cannot guarantee that a site's future contents will continue to meet our high standards of quality and educational value. Be advised that children should be closely supervised whenever they access the Internet.

INDEX